THE

MW01274694

CODEPENDENCY

or 'Rescuing the entire world all by yourself'

BY SALLY FRANZ
ILLUSTRATED BY STEVE MOLLOY

Nightingale Press

an imprint of Wimbledon Publishing Company Ltd.
LONDON

First published in Great Britain
by Wimbledon Publishing Co. Ltd
London P.O. Box 9779 SW19 7ZG

ISBN: 1 903222 39 7

Produced in Great Britain
Printed and bound in Hungary

BABY BOOMERS

Baby Boomers are everywhere. In the beginning they filled some seventy million baby strollers, then millions of dance halls doing the Lindy Hop and the Twist. At college they filled millions of administration buildings, usually in protest about how hard their life had been this far. Let's face it, they're probably the biggest group of babies the world has ever known. I should know, I'm one of them!

...And whingers. We have taken complaining to a new level. My parents were middle class, so, of course, I had to denounce them as capitalist pigs (right after they paid for my clothes, car and tuition).

I grew up under a government which guaranteed civil liberties and freedom of speech, so I used my freedom to drop out and criticize.

Inevitably, the fire of youth gradually burned out and, somewhere along the way, my life of dissolution turned into management, mortgages and materialism.

But then something even more horrible happened - I turned forty and became part of the *older generation*.

Dealing with the horror of becoming my own parents hasn't been easy. But Baby Boomers are good at re-inventing themselves. In fact, we invented the term 're-inventing yourself'!

Now we are having to admit to ourselves that

we might just be able to trust someone over thirty, or forty or fifty or, God help us, sixty! And as these rules change we find that life goes on. Though not without a few more obstacles to overcome…

So with all the enthusiasm of hurling oneself in protest over a police barrier, we strike out to the new frontiers of life as mature (or at least wrinkled) Baby Boomers.

INTRODUCTION TO CODEPENDENCY

What's all this talk about codependency? In my parents' day you just shut up and put up with a partner who was a nutter. You made your bed, you had to share it. In fact, people were happy to be unhappy in the Fifties.

It wasn't until a certain amount of unrest stirred in the political arena that people started questioning their relationships. The Baby Boomers were the first to question the purpose of living in denial. "We're staying together for the kids" was seen as a weak cry for people with no guts to live a life of personal fulfilment. Boomers started to question everything about their mediocre middle-class existence. It started with the Vietnam War, the invasion on Cambodia and what the heck those meatballs in the *Spaghetti-Whiz* cans were made of.

All of a sudden, normal codependent behaviour was thought to be deviant. It was *not* okay to cover for your loser spouse. Was your husband a boozer? Let *him* make the call to his boss. Was your wife a tart? Leave her and take the kids. No more Mr/Mrs Nice-guy. The new motto was 'tough love'. And it was probably about time.

In the past, people dealt with unpleasant things, like abuse, by blaming the victim: "Well, missy, it looks like you were just in the wrong place at the wrong time." Or denying that someone had a problem: "Hopeless gambler? No, Uncle Frank simply isn't much of a money-manager."

Now it seemed our generation had hit upon some radical new social theories: what if grown people stopped covering for each other? What if anyone over the age of thirteen could be held accountable for their own decisions and actions? What if people started making choices that resulted in their own personal happiness, and stopped blaming circumstance and surroundings for a failed life? What if people called this happiness 'good mental health', and what if everybody pursued it?

The Baby Boomers strived to shrug off the constraints which governed their parents' lives. No more excuses. No more pretending to be happy to keep the peace. No more abdicating responsibility for living their own lives. Baby Boomers started to look within for fulfilment. They became 'recovering' codependents, learning to take responsibility for their own health, happiness, and success.

Ever since self-professed codependents have been coming out of the closet, but thirty years on, there are still too many in our midst. You will recognize them if you listen. Codependents say things like "everything is fine", "let's not use ugly words", "isn't that nice", "stiff upper lip", "let a smile be your umbrella!" And so on. They do not say, "I don't like that, I want it changed, now!" or "I am not going to help you". In fact, a codependent would probably find that last sentence hard to even read!

Codependents serve everyone except themselves. But why? Well, as any good codependent knows, and I speak as an insider here, if you run everyone else's life but your own, you never have to find out if you could have made something of yourself. And there is a juicy side-benefit as well: you get to boss the hell out of people and divert so much attention towards others no one bothers to look at you.

But here's the rub: in the annals of codependency it is still a nose-to-nose tie which person is more disdainful: the sinner or the self-proclaimed saviour. So let the games begin! (If that's okay with you, of course. Otherwise we could wait, I mean, whatever you want . . .)

IDENTIFYING THE BABY BOOMER CODEPENDENTS

THE PERSONAL BANKER

Got yourself into a little gambling debt? Went wild at the mall? Just couldn't say no to the TV shopping channel? Personal banker to the rescue. He will bail you out and keep your credit rating above board. Unfortunately, he has to work three jobs to do it. But you'll pay him back ... as soon as your lucky numbers pay up on the roulette wheel!

THE NURSEMAID

Feel a bit under the weather? Go to bed - don't fight it off like the rest of us. Your nurse will bring you tea. She'll come home at lunch-time to feed you. She will use her sick days to take care of you, even though you're a grown adult. Being sick is such a pleasure with her there's hardly any reason to get better.

THE TEE TOTALLER

He comes home every night and checks the lines he made on the bottles in the drinks cabinet. He checks the trash for 'empties'. He orders you sparkling water at parties. He thinks he's so good at keeping you away from alcohol. Of course, the harder he works the harder you have to think up new ways to get booze. A dash of single malt in your insulin injections usually works pretty well.

THE EMPLOYMENT AGENT

Can't keep a job? Just can't find the right thing?
Looking perhaps for a boss who doesn't expect
you to keep regular hours and will pay you for the
days you sleep in? Just get your personal
recruitment consultant on the case. She'll scour
the want ads and classifieds, phone prospective
employers and arrange interviews. She might even
do your first day if you ask her nicely!

THE OPTIMIST

You are always so depressed and sad. But now you don't have to get a life, find out why you're angry or even go to therapy - all you need is the optimist by your side. It will be her full-time job to make you happy. Extra points for her if you don't actually *want* to be happy.

THE GUARDIAN

His job is to keep the big, bad world away from his loved ones: stop the dogs barking, silence the lawnmowers, duct tape the neighbour's kids.
All because his precious princess wants to take a nap. He is there to protect her from the harsh reality that she has to share the world with other people. Luckily, it's not so hard to keep people away any more.

THE PSYCHOLOGIST

Can't afford a therapist? Amateur psychologist to the rescue! She will listen as you pour out your heart and blame the world for your sorrows. Bonus points if she listens to the same problem over and over and sees no sign of change. She is an expert on everybody's life but her own.

THE 'DOC'

Can't sleep? The 'Doc' will give you a sample from his medicine cabinet. Who cares that the drugs he gives you are out-of-date and counter-indicated for the upper and downers you've already taken. He wants to save you the hassle of uncooperative, real doctors. The 'Doc' isn't a pusher, he's an enabler. He just wants to help.

THE SOCIAL SECRETARY

She plans parties, dinners and gatherings of any size. She writes the invitations, books the caterers, tidies up afterwards and writes the 'thank you' notes. No one can do it like she does, so she does it all by herself. But wait! The party's not over until you hear about how hard it was to do it alone.

THE CHEF

Don't like what's being served? No problem. This woman lives for picky eaters. Did she fix stuffed sole when you already had fish for lunch? Never mind, she'll barbecue ribs for you instead. Don't want oatmeal this morning? How about an omelette with ham and sausage? That only takes an extra half hour and six more pans. Just think of her as staff, not family.

THE ETERNAL MOTHER

She was a good mother: wiping noses, serving broth, folding laundry. In fact she was so helpful, kind and subservient that none of her children ever left home. Why should they? No rent, maid service, home-cooked meals. But boy, she sure is looking old for seventy.

THE BABYSITTER

Tired of your spoiled brats? Just ask the babysitter to help. She'll feed, bath and amuse your little terrors forever. She has no life and never will as long as your kids are around. Drop them off for an hour, come back next week. A box of Quality Street will make her forget that you are a complete user.

THE HEALTH FREAK

Her job is to make sure the entire family is healthy.
Exercise on the weekends, all-organic food from
the garden, yoghurt from scratch, homemade
crackers without additives. It takes her twelve
hours a day to do everything she needs. She is
going to make her family healthy if it kills her.

THE CALORIE COUNTER

She gets up at dawn to prepare fresh foods for
her fella's diet. *He* was up just before dawn
raiding the fridge. She weighs each item and
checks their nutritional values. She is slaving away
to spare her hubby a heart attack. Meanwhile,
he's dipping cheese-puffs in ice cream and chasing
them back with a beer at the local pub.

THE MEDIATOR

Family infighting is her speciality. If the Montagues and Capulets had had this woman they would have been one happy family. She listens to everyone complain and brings them all together, no matter how dysfunctional their relationships. She thinks *The Waltons* was a documentary on a real family. She is asleep on her life. Good night Johnboy. Good night reality.

THE CHARITY CASE

She is on six charity boards, bakes pies for the
church, organises the local fair and runs the
Grand Ball. You want something done, ask a busy
person. Why is all the work always done by just a
few people? Because everybody else learned how
to say NO!

THE PUSHOVER

You cheat on her, yell for no reason and complain about her cooking. She understands. She thinks if she causes you any flak, you will abandon her. What she never understands is this - if you left her, her life could actually *begin*.

THE STAGE MUM

She never had a life of her own, so now she is going to live through that of her precious baby daughter. Pierced ears, nail polish and curly wigs - all before she is two (months). She is going to make sure her daughter will get all the attention she never got. When does the daughter get her own life choices? "But this is what she wants!"

LITTLE LEAGUE DAD

This Dad is going to make sure that his son is not a sissy. Take a ball in the mouth or crotch? Hey, real men don't cry, even if they're only four. Get tough, little guy! Of course, Dad couldn't run across the field without suffering a coronary, but that's what his son's there for. You want Daddy to love you? Hit the damn ball.

THE PEACE-MAKER

She just wants everybody to kiss and makeup.
Her job is to make everybody stop feeling bad -
even if it means not feeling anything at all.
She says, "Have a nice day!" She chides her friends,
"Let's not say 'hate' or get angry". Good idea -
because if we opened up the floodgates we might
not be able to stop!

THE SCAPEGOAT

No matter who screwed up, it's this guy's fault.
He's the bad one, so what can you expect? Is
Mum a lush? He drove her to it. Is Dad a
womaniser? Yup, this guy's fault. Grandpa a lecher?
His fault again. Bad economy? Wars abroad?
Football team lost? You know who's to blame.

THE VICTIM

Life is so hard and this poor girl never gets a
break. Her boyfriend is a twit, but she'll just stay
and put up with him, because it's so hard to leave
She has 'poor me' bottled-up and ready to
market. Boss too demanding? Church too rigid?
Friends unkind? It's so hard and there's nothing
she can do about it - nothing.

THE CALL OF THE CODEPENDENT

You are not going to eat that with your hands, are you?

(Monitoring another adult's table manners started with Jane and Tarzan and has been used ever since, especially at Texas-style barbecues.)

Let me eat the burnt toast.

(Spoken by every martyr-mother alive.
Role model: Tinkerbell who drank
poison for Peter Pan.)

He needs me to help him find his way.

(Best example - Dorothy dragging her brainless,
heartless, gutless crew through Oz when *she* was
the only one who was lost.)

Why don't you eat
something? You must be
hungry. You'll be hungry
later. Okay, fine, I'll pack
you something.

(The encouragement to eat is always in
proportion to how bad the cook is.)

If I don't put up with his
temper tantrums he says
he'll leave me. I'd never find
another man to love me.

(This one is as old as the hills. I think Eve was the
first to believe there were no other men.)

Don't you want a sweater?
Let me get you a sweater,
I know you'll be cold later.

(Usually overheard at the beach in Spain in July.)

Yes, he thinks he's been
abducted by aliens forty
times, but find me a
straight man who doesn't
have a few small foibles.

(Heard on ladies nights out all over the world.)

She's not an alcoholic.
She just likes a few six
packs before bed.

(Heard from behind his evening paper.)

Don't worry, I'll protect you.

(Usually said right before the guy takes a punch
for something stupid his girlfriend said -
example: Popeye and Olive Oyl.)

If you don't give your mother grandchildren it's going to kill her.

(Your father explaining the purpose of marriage.)

What was the matter with that one, Miss Picky? You can love any man if you put your mind to it.

(Your mother explaining how she found her soul mate.)

Sex is something you do so that you can have a nice house.

(Your mother explaining economics ...
Remember codependents never ask for what they
want so good sex is a matter of chance.)

Never argue with a woman. Agree with her so you can have some peace and quiet. Then go out and do what you want to do.

(Your father explaining emotional intimacy.)

There's a right way and a wrong way to do everything.

(Black and white thinking started back with the creation of day and night. Note: this statement rarely precedes an apology.)

He's rich.

(He's an alcoholic, abusive womaniser.)

She's beautiful.

(She's an irrational prima donna.)

The child is highly strung.

(The child is a spoiled brat with an
oversized allowance.)

We are happily married
and never fight.

(We both have contracts with hit
men on each other.)

Uncle Bruce is so good with flowers!

(Uncle Bruce is a raving queer and no one but he wants to admit it.)

Auntie Jane likes to keep herself to herself.

(Auntie Jane is certifiable. She collects poisonous plants and autopsy reports of famous people.)

AUNT SASSY'S ADVICE COLUMN

The advice column to help Baby Boomers
understand the complexities of codependency.

Dear Aunt Sassy,

I love my wife, but she seems addicted to the TV shopping channel. Almost every day we get a delivery of something we don't need. I try to intercept the delivery man and send as much as I can back, but it's a losing battle. Can you help me convince her not to buy so much?

Buried in Birmingham

Dear Buried,

Shopping is a form of addiction and only *she* can deal with it. Trying to stop someone's behaviour is codependent. Stop trying to get her to stop shopping! But make sure she pays for her choices.

Another thing you might want to bear in mind: one person's trash is another person's treasure. You might think her purchases are knick-knacks and tasteless rubbish, but I bet you have a den full of sound systems and pieces of your first car. I'm sure her small purchases don't come close to what you spend on 'important' woofers, tweeters, RAM upgrades and chrome.

The real question is why do you both buy all that stuff and what would happen if you stopped collecting teapots and vintage hub caps? Dare you look that deep?

Materially yours,

AUNT SASSY

> *Dear Aunt Sassy,*
>
> *My husband likes to play golf. He gets up early and plays all day, often staying out 'til sunset. At first I thought he was having an affair and I hired a detective who said he always went straight to the golf course. I know how to compete against a well-built blonde, but how do I compete with a seven iron?*
>
> *Deserted in Daventry*

Dear Deserted,

You are what is officially known as a golf widow. Your husband's sporting obsession reflects an addictive personality and it will be difficult to get him to stop.

But about you. Only a codependent would try to compete with a seven iron. Get a grip! Isn't there something else you could be doing with your time instead of waiting in the wings for your Nick Faldo to return? You're not happy, so why not find something that will make you happy? How about playing bingo, taking up ice hockey or collecting velvet paintings of Elvis? Of course, you could always beat him at his own game. Take golf lessons and insist that you play together. That should cure him.

Swinging and putting,

AUNT SASSY

Dear Aunt Sassy,

I think my wife is a control freak. She tells me what time to get up, when to go to bed and what to wear. She nags at me all day long about table manners. She corrects my vocabulary and she yells at me in public. She was never like this when we were dating. What's happened? And what should I do about it?

Controlled in Chester

Dear Controlled,

Well, either you are a big fat slob with no social graces and few redeeming qualities, or your wife is an irate witch. I am in no position to judge. But you may want to ask yourself a few questions. When was the last time you made love, had an expensive dinner out, sent her flowers, or told her she was beautiful? Most women stop acting like dates when you stop dating them.

Here's another question. Who gets to hold the remote when watching TV? Who drives when you are together? The problem with living with a control freak is you usually don't notice unless you are one also. It's likely that you both want to tell each other what to do. You both want the other person to conform to some ideal-mate role before you'll be happy. Give it up! Decide to be happy *before* the other person changes.

And by the way, there is an easy solution to the power struggle. Take turns being in control.

You can alternate days, or pull names from a hat to choose - of course you'll have to decide whose hat to use, who puts the names in, who draws first . . .

Uncontrollably yours,

AUNT SASSY

Dear Aunt Sassy,

My husband seems glued to the TV. He watches four to six hours of sport every night. I can't get him to do any chores, walk the dog or play with the children. I beg him, nag him, sweet talk him, but to no avail. Can you tell him to move his lump off the couch and join the real world? I think he'll listen to you.

Tired in Tottenham,

Dear Tired,

Aunt Sassy is flattered that you think I can extricate your husband from the furniture, but it would take a better, if not bigger woman than me.

As I see it, there are a couple of advantages to your husband's TV watching. First of all, you always know where he is and what he's up to. Secondly, you don't have to dust the couch he's on. And finally, he's not harming anyone. It's time that you stopped putting energy into changing him. Let him sit right there and watch TV. But be creative!

Aunt Sassy knows someone who made a deal with her husband. He had to give her a back rub whenever the game was on. It got to the point where, after a long day, she would beg him to watch a few hours of sports.

Happy compromises,

AUNT SASSY

Dear Aunt Sassy,

My wife is a beautiful blue-eyed blonde. She was once a fashion model! The problem is she is so negative. Nothing is ever right. I spend all my time trying to make her happy, but it doesn't work. She screams and yells and throws things. Should I send her on a vacation to help her relax and feel better?

Drained in Doncaster

Dear Drained,

Something tells Aunt Sassy that you were so dazzled by your wife's beauty when you were dating her that you forgot to notice one little thing - she is a psycho. I believe the clinical name is manic-depressive thrombolemic - or 'loony' for short. Negative people are poison. People who try to cheer them up are codependents.

So now here's my advice. Let her stew in her own juices and go off on holiday by yourself. Why not go to a motivational convention in Hawaii? That way you can rest by the sea and be surrounded by people virtually dripping with positive attitude.

And remember: nothing puts an ex-fashion model in her place better than a husband in an orange palm-tree print T-shirt.

Positively yours,

AUNT SASSY

GUIDELINES
FOR AVOIDING
CODEPENDENCY

Codependency is a disease. And if it makes you feel better, you are not alone - it is still spreading at an alarming rate. How else can you explain the fact that airlines have added the following information to their safety manuals: 'Please secure your own oxygen mask before assisting others'? Yes - sometimes you have to tell co-dependents to remember to breathe!

But unlike the heartbreak of psoriasis or pink-eye, codependency can be contained and stopped.

One step at a time. Here are just a few words of wisdom to help you practice putting yourself first!

■ *Thanks for sharing this information, but I am not convinced that your poor choices and lack of planning makes this my problem to solve.*

■ *I'm going out to get some support and I don't mean surgical stockings or a jockstrap.*

■ *Explain to me again why your bad upbringing is the reason I should pay your gambling debts.*

■ *Apparently you believe that when you experience anger everyone around you goes deaf. Otherwise, why would you be shouting when I haven't done anything wrong?*

■ *Of course I love you. I just love me too. And if it's a toss up, I win.*

■ *If you are cooking for, doing laundry for or pampering anyone over the age of twelve you are either in love or codependent. Of those two states, codependency is probably easier to cure.*

■ *Tell me again how I qualify for being the worst parent in the world because I won't let you go out wearing a string bikini top to a dance that starts at 3am and lasts for three days.*

■ *You didn't lose your apartment because I am stingy with money; you lost your apartment because you forgot to get a job this year!*

■ *Consider this - most animals abandon their young after one year. The way I see it anything after a year is a gift, not a right.*

CONCLUSION

Codependency is when you help everybody else and ignore your own needs. It is about being so consumed with running, controlling and managing other people's lives that you feel overwhelmed by all the work. In fact, some days you feel taken for granted - which you are. Your motives might be pure, but no one appreciates all your effort. Actually, no one really needs all that much help, whether they asked for it or not.

But you're in a bit of a helping rut! You monitor your parents' drinking, your daughter's weight, your husband's driving. Then you tell strangers what to order in restaurants, you direct traffic, you take in all strays - animal and human.

In a horrible car crash when everybody else has a 'near-death' experience, codependents have a 'near-life' experience. They want to get help, but a crisis to a codependent is like a bar to an alcoholic. It's show-time! So they hobble around the crash scene blood-soaked and fainting, trying to calm the onlookers.

Fighting the urge to be a codependent takes a huge amount of energy. It means refusing to rescue people. It means letting everyone fold their own laundry. It means turning in your social police badge. Get ready! It takes a lot of practice to let go of the reins of control.

You can overcome codependency if you spend your energy taking care of yourself first. When you read a self-help book and that voice in your head says, "Oh, this would be perfect for Bob, Wendy, Joyce and Marvin", just buy one copy for yourself. And every time you want to underline a part for someone else and mail them the quote . . . don't!

Similarly, when you want to explode with advice for others on how to drive, eat, walk, dress, cook or run a business . . . don't! When you feel the urge to pick up someone else's clothes, papers, dishes, rent, gas bill, insurance . . . don't!

You can't begin to help others until you've helped yourself.

So, the cure for codependency is summed up in the saying, 'Get a Life!' Or more precisely, 'Find your own life!'